ATLANTIC
CANADA

JOSEF HANUS & JOSEF M. HANUS

Personal gift to:

From:

© *JH. Fine Art Photo Ltd.*

Cape Smokey

The colourful spring banks of Cape Smokey are one of many lovely views of Breton Island, seen while travelling along the Cabot Trail. This picture was taken from Ingonish.

Ingonish Beach

The Cape Breton Highlands National Park is located in northern Nova Scotia, on Cape Breton Island. Ingonish beach and Ingonish resort are attractive recreational centres on the eastern part of the Cabot Trail.

2

Rocky Bay

The 300 km trip around Cape Breton is a breathtaking experience. This tourist trail was named after John Cabot, who moored his ship by the island's shores in 1497. The Cabot Trail is one of the most popular hiking trails in North America. Rocky Bay is the most photographed spot on the Cabot Trail.

Cap Rouge

Beautiful green hills frame the view of the Gulf of St. Lawrence.

3

Nova Scotia

St. George's Bay

Cape Breton is separated from the mainland by the Strait of Canslo, a part of St. George's Bay. This view of the bay was taken from Cape George.

Inverness

Inverness is a fishing village along the Cabot Trail, and is well known for its sunny beaches.

Nova Scotia

Cape Breton Island

This island, located at the northernmost part of Nova Scotia, was first explored by John Cabot in 1497. Its magnificent natural beauty is a major attraction on Cape Breton. Almost 300 km of modern two-lane highway is popular with cyclists, and numerous trails and campsites offer relaxation time in the park to motorists travelling around Nova Scotia.

Nova Scotia

Cape North

A spectacular view of Pleasant Bay, the northern part of Cape Breton Island and Red River can be seen from the view point high above White Capes. Whale watching is a popular tourist attraction all around the northern part of Cape Breton Island.

Pleasant bay

6

Thompson Pass

The northernmost part of the Cabot Trail Highway passes 'Lone Shieling', located in the forest near Pleasant Bay.

Aspy Bay

Nova Scotia

St. Anns Bay

The eastern part of Cape Breton Island has many beautiful spots. St. Anns Bay, Wreck Cove, French River and Indian Brook are favourite tourist stops along the Cabot Trail.

Sydney

A relatively small city and mining centre, Sydney is the third largest community in Nova Scotia. Founded in 1785 by Loyalists, Sydney is now the commercial and industrial centre of Cape Breton Island.

8

Nova Scotia

Sydney Heritage

The old architecture of numerous buildings and churches in Sydney is an irresistible attraction for visitors. St. Patrick church, renovated later into a museum, was built in 1828 from the stones of Louisbourg ruins. St. George's Church is one of Canada's oldest Anglican churches.

Cossitt House

Cossitt House, built in 1874, is the oldest remaining residence in Sydney.

9

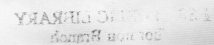

Pictou

180 Scottish colonists came here in 1773 in the bark *Hector*, but the first settlement began in June 1767 with the arrival of six families from Maryland and Pennsylvania. Several historic homes and the reconstructed bark *Hector* are shown here. Pictou is a ferry port, connecting Nova Scotia and Prince Edward Island, across Northumberland Strait.

10

Nova Scotia

Fortress Louisbourg

The Fortress of Louisbourg, France's bastion of military strength, was built 1714–1744 on the eastern point of Cape Breton Island. Louisbourg was captured by the British in 1758 and was later destroyed in 1760. Louisbourg is now Canada's largest historic reconstruction. The three-storey King's Bastion Barracks, home to the 500 French soldiers who lived here, and the port's defence post are pictured here. Louisbourg National Historic Site is one of the more popular historic sites in Nova Scotia.

11

Nova Scotia

Dartmouth

A. Murray McKay Bridge, high above The Narrows and Bedford Basin Bay, connects the two largest cities of Nova Scotia—Halifax and Dartmouth. Another modern bridge that spans the harbour is the Angus L. Macdonald Bridge. The Dartmouth port is in the second photograph.

12

Port of Halifax

Over 3,500 ships dock in the Port of Halifax annually. The port is busiest in the winter because it is ice free while ports along the St. Lawrence Seaway are frozen over. The harbour is 1.5 km wide and Ports Ocean Terminals provide ample space for the largest of freighters. Halifax Port is connected with Dartmouth by North America's oldest town ferry.

13

Nova Scotia

Remembering the Titanic

The disaster of the Titanic sinking on April 14, 1912 touched the city of Halifax deeply. 125 victims of the tragedy were laid to rest at the Fairview Cemetery in Halifax, about 900 miles away from the place where the 'unsinkable' vessel sank after its collision with a huge iceberg. The iceberg in this picture is of a similar size to the one which sank the S.S. Titanic.

14

Nova Scotia

Halifax Explosion

The biggest non-nuclear blast ever happened in Halifax Harbour after the French munitions ship Mont Blanc collided with a Norwegian freighter. It happened on December 6, 1917. The explosion killed over 1,600 people. The anchor of the Mont Blanc broke into two pieces and flew over 4 kilometres from Halifax Harbour. A memorial was erected on the site where the 300 kilogram anchor shaft was found.

THE
DEC. 6
1917
HALIFAX
EXPLOSION
HURLED THIS
1140 LB ANCHOR
SHAFT 2.35 MILES
FROM THE S.S. MONT
BLANC TO THIS PARK.

Nova Scotia

Halifax Downtown

Situated around Citadel Hill, Halifax the capital of Nova Scotia was founded in 1749 by General G. Cornwallis and 2,500 English settlers. A small romantic city with 250 years of history, it has five universities and is Nova Scotia's largest urban centre, and Atlantic Canada's cultural and shopping capital. A walk around the harbour is a pleasant way to experience a panorama of Halifax .

16

Nova Scotia

Halifax Citadel

Halifax Citadel was built in 1828–1856, in a star-shaped design, to defend the city, which was never attacked. Daily, thousands of visitors can view museum displays of furniture, the centennial art gallery and can explore military exhibits, powder magazines and secret firing rooms.

Old Town Clock

A Halifax landmark, the Old Town Clock was built in 1803 on Citadel Hill as a gift from Edward, the Duke of Kent.

Nova Scotia

Fisheries Museum

A main Lunenburg attraction is the Fisheries Museum of the Atlantic. An aquarium, a collection of small marine engines, numerous vessels moored in the vessel gallery, and more, attract many visitors daily, travelling around Nova Scotia from Halifax and Peggy's Cove to Yarmouth. The museum originally began aboard the Theresa E. Connor in 1967.

18

Nova Scotia

Lunenburg

A popular tourist stop on the Atlantic Ocean, Lunenburg is located between Mahone Bay and Lunenburg Harbour, just 80 km west of Peggy's Cove. The port was settled in 1780 by Swiss, German and French immigrants. The colourful 'old town' Lunenburg, a UNESCO World Heritage Site, is the home port of the Bluenose II schooner and the Fisheries Museum.

19

Nova Scotia

Peggy's Cove

The most popular Nova Scotian tourist destination, Peggy's Cove was named after the archangel Peggy, the sole survivor of a terrible 19th century shipwreck. Thousands of tourists stroll daily amongst the granite rocks around the lighthouse, and visit numerous restaurants, offering a very unique dish, Atlantic Lobster. The picturesque and colourful cove with old port buildings and numerous fishing boats make aesthetic subjects for photographers and painters.

20

St. Margaret's Bay

The fishing village of Peggy's Cove, situated by the mouth of St. Margaret's Bay, is the home of the most famous lighthouse in Canada, standing on wave-worn granite rocks.

Flight memorial

The memorial of Swissair Flight 111 is close to Peggy's Cove. Two large boulders are placed to indicate where the aircraft and its 265 passengers plunged into the icy waters of the Atlantic Ocean.

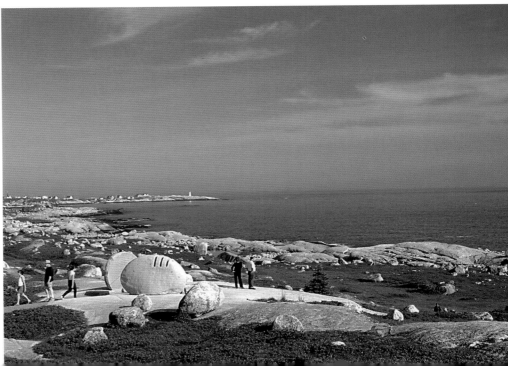

21

Nova Scotia

Five Islands

Minas Basin, a part of Cobequit Bay, is home to Five Islands Provincial Park. Red sandy hiking trails around 40 metre high cliffs of Minas Basin are popular weekend destinations.

Port Hood

St. Peter's Church in Port Hood, close to Invermere.

Nova Scotia

Yarmouth

The city of Yarmouth, once the richest port on the Atlantic Coast, is situated in the western part of Nova Scotia. Yarmouth is well known for its shipbuilding during the Golden Age of sailing ships in the late 19th century. This community was settled by Acadians in 1768. Some architectural examples remain in the city, which today is a popular destination and ferry port to Portland and Bar Harbour in Maine, USA.

Nova Scotia

Shelburne

The shipbuilding town of Shelburne was founded by loyalists in 1783. The Dory Shop Museum (smaller picture) and several other historic homes, such as Ross-Thompson House built in 1784, were restored as a branch of the Nova Scotia Museum. This quiet historic town is nestled deep in the harbour.

Jordan River

The larger picture on this page is of Jordan River, photographed near Jordan Falls.

24

Confederation Bridge

At 13 km long, *The Link* is the world's longest multispan bridge. It connects Prince Edward Island with New Brunswick. The 900 million dollar bridge, completed in May 1997, gave tourists a simple way to the island and provided year-round commercial transport across the ice-covered waters of Northumberland Strait during winter. Gateway Village offers an info centre, gift shops, restaurants, and a statue of Anne of Green Gables. Gateway is the first stop after arriving in P.E.I. The trip to the Island, using the bridge or ferry in Wood Islands is *free of charge!* Travellers have only to pay for the return trip.

25

Prince Edward Island

Canada's Settlement

Charlottetown, the capital of Prince Edward Island, is known as the birthplace of Canada. In September 1864, the first meeting of the Canadian Confederation took place here. The picture of the park and War Monument was taken in a park near Province House.

Province House

Built in the Georgian style, in 1843–1847, Province House is now known as the Confederation Chamber. Today it is home to the P.E.I. Legislative Assembly.

Prince Edward Island

Charlottetown

Elegant city streets characterize Canada's smallest provincial capital and the only large city on Prince Edward Island, nestled in Charlottetown Harbour, on the shores of Northumberland Strait. Charlottetown was settled by the British in 1794.

27

Prince Edward Island

French River

A colourful landscape, stitched together with rivers and lakes used for oyster farming, is a magnet for tourists. In this picture is a fishing community near Cavendish, called French River.

Indian River

St. Mary's Roman Catholic Church shines brilliantly in the island landscape. The village of Indian River is situated by Baie Malpeque Bay, near Cabot Beach Provincial Park.

28

Borden Beach

Northumberland Strait has numerous sunny beaches. This sunset picture of Borden Beach was taken close to the Confederation Bridge.

Cavendish Beach

Beaches around Prince Edward Island are very different, but all are beautiful. The sand near Cavendish is tinted pink by the erosion of bleached red clay. Windy beaches with red sandstone cliffs around North Cape are famous among windsurfers and sailors. Swimmers and sunbathers prefer the beaches on the island's south side. These are much sought after for their warm, pleasing climate.

29

Prince Edward Island

Cavendish

Cavendish is home to Green Gables, and the location of Lucy Maud Montgomery's famous novel, *Anne of Green Gables*. This beautiful place is visited by almost all visitors to Prince Edward Island.

Avonlea

Built in the architectural style of early Prince Edward Island, the village of Anne of Green Gables is another historic stop on the way around P.E.I. Long River Church was actually attended by L.M. Montgomery, and she was baptized here in 1875.

30

West Point

Cedar Dunes Provincial Park is the home of West Point Lighthouse. Red sandstone cliffs eroded by wind and water are characteristic of the most westerly part of P.E.I. The black and white striped lighthouse is a one-of-a-kind on the island. This part, washed by the waters of Baie Egmont Bay, is known as Sunsets & Seascapes.

Summerside

The quiet town of Summerside, located in Bedeque Bay 60 km west of Charlottetown, is known for its summer festival, with a step-dancing contest, the crowning of Miss P.E.I. and lobster suppers.

Prince Edward Island

Lobster & Potatoes

True to the title of this page, two main activities are all around you while travelling across Prince Edward Island. Abundant potato fields and fishing boats exist side-by-side. Lobster traps by the hundreds are in each port and by the side of many houses.

Wood Islands

The ferry connecting Prince Edward Island with Nova Scotia's Pictou has its terminal in Wood Islands. This picture was taken in the fishing port of Wood Islands.

32

Murray Head

The shores of Prince Edward Island are blessed with miles of warm sandy beaches, changing into dunes and rugged cliffs, offering photographers beautiful sunny scenery. Murray Head, the subject of this picture, is situated by the mouth of Murray Harbour in the eastern part of the island.

North Lake

Fishing village of North Lake is situated near East Point. This area is famous for the biggest tuna fish.

33

Victoria Harbour

The fishing wharf of Victoria is situated near Hampton.

Cape Bear

The distress signal from the Titanic was first received at the radio station on Cape Bear. The lighthouse is in the smaller picture.

34

Point Wolfe

The rugged shoreline of Fundy National Park creates dramatic fjords. Point Wolfe River is located close to Alma.

Magnetic Hill

Magnetic Hill, first popularized in 1933, located close to Moncton, is known as a motorist and tourist attraction. The road appears to go uphill, but the opposite is true. Motorists can check out this illusion, coasting up-hill in neutral for just two dollars.

35

New Brunswick

Moncton

Historical buildings and streets attract visitors to the second largest city in New Brunswick. Moncton is an important industrial and cultural centre. *Université de Moncton* is the only French language university located east of Québec. Historical interest points include Moncton Civic Museum, the Free Meeting House, the Capital Theatre and the Acadian Museum.

36

Parlee Beach

Parlee Beach is one of many warm sunny beaches located on the shores of Northumberland Strait and the Gulf of the St. Lawrence. Heavily occupied beaches, located east of Moncton, are known as Florida North.

Robichaud

The fishing wharf Robichaud is located near Cape Pélé and Murray Beach Provincial Park, on the shore of Northumberland Strait.

37

Bay of Fundy

A vibrant place for all tourists travelling across New Brunswick is Fundy National Park. The 207-square kilometre park is located on the eastern shore of the province. Its waters are coloured a deep red and are never clear, because of great rapids of low and high tides in this area.

Alma

The biggest rapids between high and low tides are in Alma, a small community located on the eastern end of the park, in Rocher Bay. Colourful rock specimens can be found at low tide by the mouth of Salmon River.

38

New Brunswick

The Rocks

The Rocks Provincial Park is world-famous for its tidal wonders. Billions of litres of water move twice a day in the Bay of Fundy, creating an incredible difference of 15 metres between low and high tide. Small islands in the first photograph are transformed by the low tide into tall rocks, resembling flower-pots (second picture). Swirling tides with nutrient-rich waters attract numerous species such as minke, finback and the world's largest population of whales.

39

New Brunswick

Saint John

Saint John is one of North America's oldest cities. Explorer Samuel de Champlain anchored in the harbour in 1604 and named the Saint John River. A trading post was established here in 1631 and early English settlement dates back to 1762. The main influx of settlers was of several thousand Loyalists from the United States in 1783. Saint John is now a shipping, mining and industrial city. The modern downtown was photographed from across the harbour, where the river empties into the Bay of Fundy. The second photo was taken from Westmorland Heights.

40

Reversing Falls

The Saint John River, emptying into Grand Bay and Bay of Fundy, creates powerful rapids twice a day, when the sea pushes the river back into the narrow and deep gorge.

Saint John Harbour

A principal seaport, Saint John is the oldest incorporated city in Canada. The city's harbour was photographed from Loyalist Landing Place.

41

New Brunswick

Saint John Downtown

Market Square is Saint John's festival place. Facing the scenic Bay of Fundy, Brunswick Square and Market Place are charming relaxing places for locals and tourists alike. Unique goods can be purchased in Atlantic Canada's longest indoor, climate controlled pedestrian walkway system.

New Brunswick

Hammondvale

This view of a Christmas tree farm was photographed near Hammondvale, in New Brunswick.

Petit-Roche

43

Village Acadien

Village Historique Acadien shows a rural Acadian community between 1770-1890. The village has 45 restored buildings and covers 900 acres. Visitors can see life in the village as it would have been in the 19th century. Costumed guides re-create daily activities such as blacksmithery, printing and day-to-day life on the farm.

New Brunswick

Saint John River

River Valley Scenic Drive follows the valley along Saint John River, from Saint John and Fredericton to Edmundston. Cross the world's longest covered bridge, the dramatic Grand Falls and visit the capital city with its 19th century charms, and finally stop in Saint John, by the Bay of Fundy.

St. Anne de Madagaska

45

King's Landing

This historical settlement, situated on the banks of St. John River, vibrantly re-creates rural life in 19th century New Brunswick. Many restored historic homes were moved from different places into this village, named King's Landing. Costumed staff work diligently to accurately portray an important era in Canadian history. Thousands of visitors enjoy strolls in this beautiful village close to Fredericton.

Fredericton Heritage

The Old Government House, the Georgian style home of New Brunswick Lieutenant-Governors was built in 1826-1828.

City Hall

Fredericton's City Hall was built in 1876. It is Atlantic Canada's oldest city hall still in use. Fredericton, the capital of New Brunswick, was settled in 1783.

47

New Brunswick

Fredericton

The silver-domed Victorian New Brunswick Legislative Building is situated by the bank of St. John's River. Built in 1880, the building is the most celebrated New Brunswick historic site. In the smaller picture on this page are the streets of Fredericton's downtown.

New Brunswick

Shippegan

Situated on the Acadian Peninsula, the fishery town Shippegan is known for its July Fisheries Festival. Fishing trips, street dancing and delicious seafood platters are magnetic for tourists travelling through Atlantic Canada.

Caracus

Small town near Fredericton.

49

New Brunswick

St. Michael's Basilica

The imposing gothic structure of St. Michael's Basilica, situated on the hill above Miramichi, was built in 1839. The religious history of the Miramichi area begins in the early part of the 18th century, when Missionaries from Québec visited and ministered to early settlers. By the late 1790's there were enough Roman Catholics to establish a church.

50

Miramichi Bay

The Miramichi River is world famous for the Atlantic salmon which populate its waters. Miramichi is home to Canada's First Irish Festival, Agricultural Exhibition, Folk Song Festival and Rock 'n' Roll Festival, all held in the summer months. Manderson Beach is open to swimmers and hosts numerous attractions such as Parlee Beach, Acadian Historic Village, Magic Mountain, Whale watching or Kouchibougac Park, all 30 minutes to two hour trips from here.

Campbellton

A large New Brunswick seaport and the north shore's commercial centre.

51

New Brunswick

Sussex countryside

Beautiful agricultural scenery is all around, travelling from Sussex to the Bay of Fundy, New Brunswick's most visited national park.

Sussex

A small town located south of Moncton, Sussex is the last stop when travelling to Fundy National Park and to the Rocks, the famous place of the biggest tides.

Pokeshaw Island

Pokeshaw Island, a favourite spot of photographers and the home of thousand of seabirds, is located in Chaleur Bay, near Bertrand and Caraquet Provincial Park.

Grande-Anse

Located in Chaleur bay, Grande-Anse beaches are popular for locals and tourists.

53

New Brunswick

Grand Falls

Travelling from Edmundston south to Fredericton, Grand Falls are a favourite stop for tourists.

Edmundston

The pulp-producing centre of Edmundston, located in the upper St. John River Valley, was named after Governor Sir Edmund Head.

Cartwright

The fishing village of Cartwright, located on the shore of the Atlantic Ocean, is the only stop on the ferry connecting Newfoundland's Lewisport with Labrador's Goose Bay. Cartwright is the fishing centre of small villages on the Labrador coast.

Red Bay

Seen across Red Bay, a historic village is located at the end of route 510. This part of Labrador can be reached by the seasonal ferry from St. Barbe to Blanc-Sablon. An old fishing village and the first fish factory in the New World, it was inhabited in the 16th century by Basque whalers.

55

Groswater Bay

Labrador is known as the last pristine wilderness in North America. A coastal ferry travels with visitors and locals six days from St. Anthony to Nain and then six days back, stopping in numerous small villages on the shore of the Labrador Sea.

St. Mary's

The village of St. Mary's Harbour, nestled in Gilbert Bay can be easily reached by a new gravel highway from Red Bay. With private boats, tourists can easily visit the most popular spot in Labrador, Battle Harbour. The former residents of Battle Harbour now live in the village of St. Mary's.

56

Labrador

Battle Harbour

In the last century, Battle Harbour was known for its salted Cod trade, and was home to several hundred fishermen and their families. Once the unofficial capital of Labrador (1870-1930), Battle Harbour is now a museum of the bygone era. In the church, everything is as if people left this place yesterday. Looking into the houses, there are dishes and bread on the tables. Two decades ago, the dwindling population was relocated to St. Mary's. The homes are maintained by several families and a small hotel provides lodging for several visitors daily. Tourists can stroll the island and get a taste of the way life was in coastal Labrador a century ago.

57

Labrador

Labrador City

Atlantic Canada's most northern city is located on the Quebec-Labrador border, in the midst of ancient tundra. The town is situated on the middle point of the thousand kilometre long Labrador Highway, which connects Goose Bay with Baie-Comeau in Quebec. This modern city is home to ten thousand people, mostly interested in the business of iron mining.

Winokapau Lake

Winokapau Lake is located 90 km west of Labrador City. 300,000 square kilometres of unspoiled land in Labrador attract hunters and anglers from around the world. Labrador's pristine rivers and lakes are known as a sportsman's paradise. Western Labrador is home to 700 000 caribou. Labrador is a land where paleo-indigenous people lived 9,000 years ago.

Muskrat Falls

Located close to Happy Valley, Muskrat Falls are the part of Churchill River just before it empties into Lake Melville.

59

Labrador

Churchill Falls

Churchill River, creating dramatic views with its rocky river bed, flows from Smallwood Reservoir into Lake Melville. The town of Churchill Falls is located half way between Labrador City and Happy Valley. It is the only community on this part of the Labrador Highway, where travellers can stop and rest after travelling a long, sometimes very rough highway.

60

Goose Bay/Happy Valley

For drivers finally reaching the largest town in the wilderness of Central Labrador, the names of Happy Valley and Goose Bay are music to the ears, after the long trip across Labrador. As well as the Labrador Heritage Museum and the Moravian Church, the town has an important ferry port, connecting Labrador with Newfoundland's Lewisporte. The ferry trip is almost 45 hours long and having a reservation is very important.

61

Labrador

Trans-Labrador Highway

The Trans-Labrador Highway, constructed from 1965-1992, connects Happy Valley/Goose Bay with Wabush and Labrador City and then with Quebec's Fermont and Baie-Comeau. This well-maintained gravel highway travells past beautiful places, lakes and rivers. Thousands of tourists from North America travel along Labrador Highway to the Coastal Ferries, to explore the wildest part of Eastern Canada. Caribou 600,000 strong inhabit the George River. The largest black bear and bald eagle populations in North America can be seen in Labrador.

Labrador

Labrador scenery

There is no other place in Canada like the Labrador wilderness, a paradise for photographers, anglers and tourists exploring this part of Atlantic Canada. A coastal ferry with 48 stops in 12 days brings visitors into Nain, where Moravian missionaries first stationed in Labrador in 1771. British physician W. Grenfell opened the first medical facility for Inuit and fishermen in 1893, in Battle Harbour. Canada's largest hydroelectric plant was constructed on Churchill River, bringing to the region a 5,400,500-kilowatt generating capacity.

63

Labrador Sea

The most exciting part of the trip across Labrador is sailing on the Labrador Sea. This picture was taken near Battle Harbour from the ferry that connects Happy Valley/Goose Bay with Lewisporte. Hundreds of blue icebergs attract travellers during the two day trip to Newfoundland. Whale watching is common by the shores of Labrador and on hundreds another places around the island. And above the sea - the Northern Lights plays to the audience on 240 nights a year.

Avalon Peninsula

Travelling to Canada's largest island via a ferry from Sydney to Argentia, the way across the island starts along the Avalon Peninsula. Beautiful and wide countryside of green plains coloured by tiny summer cottages, a deep blue ocean dotted by white icebergs and fishing boats, fresh air and friendly people are the first impressions of this Canadian island, aptly named *'New-found-land'*.

Ferryland

The small community of Ferryland, located on the east side of Avalon Peninsula is connected with the English explorer Lord Baltimore, who anchored here in 1621, with 11 settlers.

65

Newfoundland

St. Mary's Bay

The shore of the Atlantic Ocean and St. Mary's Harbour is a place of final rest for the original European settlers in Newfoundland. Some of them were born in the 16th century, as is recorded on some tombstones framed by the grass.

Isle-aux-Morts

A fishing village near Channel-Port aux Basques, it is a ferry port connecting Newfoundland with Sydney in Nova Scotia.

Bonavista

A fascinating community and one of the oldest settlements is located on the top of Bonavista Peninsula. This popular tourist spot in Newfoundland is the largest all-fishing town in the province. A beautiful historic town is the centre for tourists visiting the lighthouse and beaches, where John Cabot moored his vessel five hundred years ago.

Newfoundland

Blackhead Bay

Cape Bonavista is believed to be the point where the Italian explorer John Cabot first stepped ashore in the 'New World'. Over 17,000 kilometres of rugged coastline of Labrador and Newfoundland offer spectacular views.

John Cabot

A stone statue of explorer John Cabot, who stepped on the shore in 1497, is placed near the lighthouse.

68

Newfoundland

Bonavista Bay

Beaches and rocks on the shores of Bonavista Bay are configured in very unique formations. Flat stone beaches around the town of Bonavista change by the tip of Bonavista Cape into dramatic stone formation-as shows this picture.

Cabot's ship

A replica of Cabot's original vessel, which the explorer anchored by the shores of Bonavista half a millennium ago, was built in a Bonavista Port for tourist and cruising purposes.

69

Spillars Cove

The eastern part of Cape Bonavista and the green Atlantic Ocean are alluring to tourists visiting the most striking part of the rugged coast in Newfoundland.

Bonavista Lighthouse

This lighthouse was built on the spot where John Cabot first landed in the New World.

70

St. John's Water Street

Water Street is North America's oldest street. Colourful buildings and small houses around the downtown of the capital city of Newfoundland are typical of the city, spread on the shores of the most easterly part of Canada. Some streets of St. John's are considered the oldest streets in North America. The city is home to Newfoundland Museum, the Memorial University of Newfoundland, many historical buildings and churches as Old Garrison Church and the Basilica of St. John the Baptist.

71

Newfoundland

St. John's

Once Britain's oldest colony and North America oldest city, St. John's is the capital of Newfoundland, the youngest Canadian province. The city is situated in the Avalon Region on the shores of Atlantic Ocean. St. John's is a city of contrast. Modern architecture in downtown spreads back along some of the oldest streets. Newly constructed buildings stand side by side with the historic houses of the oldest North American street, Water Street.

72

St. John's Harbour

The capital city of Newfoundland has a rich history. Sir Humphrey Gilbert claimed Britain's first Colony in 1583. Early settlers built houses around Newfoundland's bays in 1500. John Cabot moored his vessel in 1497 and in 1665 the French and Dutch burned and plundered the town. In 1762 the British regained the town, which was destroyed by fire in 1892 and rebuilt again. The pictures show a general view of the area around the city and port.

Newfoundland

Signal Hill

Rising 150 metres above sea level, National Historic Park of Signal Hill is the most famous spot in the St. John's area. The Queen's Battery was built after a 1762 battle, to protect the entrance to St. John's Harbour. The first transatlantic wireless message was received here, on Signal Hill by Gugliemo Marconi in December 1901. Cabot Tower was built atop a rocky hill to commemorate John Cabot's discovery of Newfoundland in 1497.

74

South Head

Situated strategically by the mouth of St. John's Harbour, South Head was an important point of Canada's defence system in the World War II. There is a very clear view of the rocky post from Signal Hill.

75

Atlantic Ocean

During the last millennium, the rough and cold Atlantic Ocean was the only access to North America for explorers and early settlers. The explorers Cabot and Columbus were guided across the Atlantic with astrolabes. The first transatlantic flight was in 1919 from St. John's to Ireland. The distance to Ireland from this point is shorter than the distance to Ontario's Thunder Bay.

Cape Spear

A memorial of World War II sits on the sandy rocks of Cape Spear.

Newfoundland

Cape Spear

Fixed on the most easterly point in North America, Cape Spear Lighthouse is a symbol of Newfoundland's independence, and is located just 10 km southeast of St. John's. Two lighthouses sit on the rocky cliffs, washed roughly by the waters of the cold sea. A breathtaking view of the Atlantic Ocean, good possibilities for whale watching, the War Memorial, and a simply relaxing place high above the water level are irresistible for tourists.

77

King's Cove

A small fishing town, King's Cove is located by Hwy 230, known as the 'Discovery Trail', above the Black Head Bay, on the Bonavista Peninsula. Peter and Paul Catholic Church was established in 1815.

Heart's Content station

The first relay station in North America was Newfoundland's end of the Transatlantic telegraph cable, linking the island with Ireland's Valentia. 2,400 km of cable was placed on the ocean floor by the world's largest steamship, S.S. Great Eastern in 1866. The red brick station was closed after 92 years in service and in 1972 was re-opened as a museum.

78

Deer Cove

The rocky eastern shores of Newfoundland, close to Gros Morne National Park, are washed by the dark blue waters of the Gulf of St. Lawrence in this picture.

Petty Harbour

Avalon Peninsula, on the eastern part of Newfoundland, is the home of countless romantic fishing villages. Close to St. John's in Cochrane Pond Prov. Park in Sohal Bay is nestled small and lovely Petty Harbour, several kilometres from Cape Spear, the easternmost point in Canada and North America.

79

Newfoundland

Twillingate

The fishing villages of Durrell and Twillingate are located on the most northern tip of New World Island. A scenic 100 km trip from Notre-Dame Junction through Jonathan's and Didlo Run Provincial Park by Hwy 340 will lead tourists into romantic Twillingate. Old tombstones by St. Peter's Anglican Church are silent memorials to the first settlers of this village. The second picture shows the village.

Durrell

The fishing village of Durrell is located in Wild Cove, close to Twillingate and Gillesport. Durrell is one of the more frequented villages on New World Island.

81

Arnold's Cove

Arnold's Cove is located by Hwy #1, deep-set in Placentia Bay.

Terra Nova

The Provincial Park Terra Nova is located between the Eastern and Avalon regions of Newfoundland. This picture was taken in Clode Sound. Newfoundland is an island of 150,000 moose. There is fantastic fishing in countless brooks and lakes on the island. Common catch are brookies, at about 7 pounds each.

Newfoundland

Bay de Verde

The picturesque village Bay de Verde is located on the northern point of the Bay de Verde Peninsula, on the shore of the Conception Bay. This is one of the most romantic spots in Newfoundland and should not be missed when travelling across the island.

Red Head Cove

A small community named Red Head Cove is located on the northern tip of Bay de Verde Peninsula.

83

St. Anthony

Travelling by Hwy #430 along Northern Peninsula, the last community on the highway and the most northern point of the peninsula is St. Anthony. This small town located in Hare Bay is a rallying point for groups protesting the seal hunt.

Daniels Harbour

Numerous small harbours are located on the eastern shore of the Northern Peninsula.

84

L'Anse aux Meadows

This Viking settlement on the top of the Northern Peninsula is the only Viking settlement in North America. In about A.D. 850, Norwegians began to explore the North Atlantic. A settlement of Vinland in Norse sagas was believed to have been established in L'Anse aux Meadows 1000 years ago. A Norwegian archeological team discovered remains of seven buildings and several household articles similar to those found in North Europe and Greenland. Eight reconstructed buildings in this National Historic Site have guides in traditional dress to take visitors back to A.D. 1000.

85

Newfoundland

Gros Morne

Northern Peninsula is home to the most popular park in Newfoundland, Gros Morne. Long Range Mountains here rise over 700 meters and the highest point is Gros Morne with its 806 m, the second highest point in Newfoundland. A 2000 square kilometre park, nestled by the Gulf of St. Lawrence, it has the world's largest caribou habitat, 170 bird species and a thousand moose, along with many other species. Gros Morne is photographed in the first picture. The second picture is of the Western Brook gorge.

86

Flowers Cove

Romantic shores with old fishing cottages are everywhere, travelling along the Northern Peninsula to St. Anthony and St. Barbe, where a ferry port transports tourists and locals to Quebec's Blanc-Sablon and to Labrador.

Long Range Mountains

The Long Range Mountains wind completely across the eastern part of Newfoundland. This picture was taken by Portland Creek.

Newfoundland

Bonne Bay

Bonne Bay and Lobster Cove, in this sunset picture, are situated in the centre of Gros Morne National Park.

Lobster Cove Head

A lighthouse called *Lobster Cove Head* is located on the rocks above Bonne Bay in Gros Morne Provincial Park. An ethereal view of the Bonne Bay and the Gulf of St. Lawrence can be found from this place. Photographs on this page were our last shots taken during the long and beautiful trip across Newfoundland, before boarding the ferry connecting Newfoundland's Port-aux-Basques with Sydney in Nova Scotia.

88